Before **SELMA**

The Harry T. Moore Story™

By

T0204634

Florence Alexander, Ph. D.

Before SELMA
The Harry T. Moore Story™

Alexander, Florence, 1938
Before SELMA...The Harry T. Moore Story
Includes color illustrations
ISBN 978-0-91596-06-4

Publication Data

Alexander, Florence, African Americans, Biography, Civil Rights, Justice, Martyr, Education, History, Civil Rights History, Black History, Black, Slavery, Middle Passage, KKK, Ku Klux Klan, White Supremacy, Lynching, Burning, Discrimination, Racial Discrimination

Published by Ebon Research Systems Publishing
P.O. Box 915115
Longwood, FL 32791
USA
Telephone: 407-682-6744
Fax: 407=774-5204
Email: Femillionaire@embarqmail.com

This book is dedicated to Jaunita Evangeline Moore, *"Daddy's Girl"* (below) who was the lookout *"through the back window"* and works tirelessly as an adult to bring about the recognition of the contribution of her parents, Harry T. and Harriette V. Moore, who gave their lives in the struggle of freedom and justice for all peoples.

3

Before SELMA, there was Harry T. Moore

The quiet, still silence was suddenly broken by the loud, piecing noise of the bomb that exploded in Mims, Florida on a foggy Christmas night December 25, 1951.   Boom!!!

Before the blast, the peaceful wedding anniversary celebration was a welcomed diversion to the trials and tribulations of this civil rights leader and his wife in the deep southern town. Before the blast, the modest Moore home was nestled in the Orange Groves of this small town and was full of Christmas decorations, presents and delicious food.   Before the blast, Harry, Harriett, Peaches and Harry's mother, Rosalea, said their prayers and went to bed in their sparsely furnished shotgun home. Before the blast, life for white southerners in Florida changed drastically because of the uncompromising courage of this gentle, slight-built man.

Against all odds and with death staring him in the face at every turn, the shy Harry T. Moore charged ahead, with his wife and children at his side, in his quest to make a difference in the quality of life for his people.   The impact of this brave, great civil rights martyr changed forever the course of history for people of color. His footprint will be felt for many years to come in America and around the world. In the immortal words of Harry T. Moore, he summarized his life's work as "this great struggle to secure for our people a fuller enjoyment of their Constitutional rights and privileges." It is on the shoulders of Harry T. Moore that we all stand today.

The blast silenced his corporal voice, but his words ring out today as a beacon for all to follow for freedom and world peace.

How Did the World Produce a Harry T. Moore?

This story begins on the coast of the Dark Continent, Africa. Africans from the regions of Senegambia, Upper Guinea, Windward Coast, Gold Coast, Bight of Benin, Bight of Biafra, West Central Africa and Southeastern Africa were captured, imprisoned in slave castles for months and finally taken to slave ships through what became known in recent times as the *"Door of No Return."* The slave ships traversed the long journey through the Middle Passage to the Americas and the Caribbean.

The Africans were enslaved primarily by Europeans. Initially, the Portuguese, Dutch and English were involved in the slave trade. The English were followed soon thereafter by other Europeans from Spain, France, Denmark, Sweden and the Netherlands. The Middle Passage voyage claimed the lives of millions of Africans due to widespread diseases caused by grossly unsanitary conditions, malnutrition, the introduction of foreign germs from Europeans and various forms of brutal treatment. Those Africans who survived the most inhumane treatment brought to the Americas a strong gene pool and the determination to survive under the harshest of conditions.

In 1619, the twenty slaves who arrived in Jamestown, Virginia were sold as the first slaves in the British North American colonies. Harry T. Moore's ancestors were survivors of the Middle Passage, and so, his origin in America began.

Slavery spread rapidly from Virginia, to the Carolinas and Georgia, then eventually into Florida. The slaves who came to Florida were runaway slaves seeking freedom. The brave slaves who fled the Carolinas and migrated to Florida sought land where they could preserve their culture and at the same time assimilate to some extent with the Spanish who occupied the northern portion of the state, today known as St. Augustine. A proud runaway slave assumed the leadership role and formed a crew of slaves with construction skills for the building of Fort Moses.

Within the walls of Fort Moses, runaway slaves planted corn and other vegetables. They built wood frame houses that provided shelter for more than 100 slaves. The Fort Moses slaves gained an enviable reputation for being a fearless bunch as they helped the Spanish in wars against the English who attempted from time to time to capture the land from the Spanish. The leader of the slaves received recognition from the Spanish government for his bravery and command qualities as he led the slave troops into battle. The slave leader learned to read and write with the assistance of early Spanish settlers. He used his familiarity with Spanish procedures to write a letter to the Spanish Governor requesting freedom for all of the slaves who fought against the English. After several letters and a change in the administration resulting from a new Governor being voted into office, the Spanish approved his request and gave the Fort Moses slaves who fought with him their freedom.

Following the unprecedented decision regarding the Fort Moses slave soldiers, the Spanish Government relaxed laws for other runaway slaves who reached Florida. Under Spanish rule, Fort Moses slaves and former slaves were allowed to intermarry with Spanish, received pay for their services and were baptized into the Christian religion. Unlike the other slave states, Florida had the distinction that in 1731 the Spanish reversed an earlier 1730 decision and declared that slaves fleeing to Florida from the Carolinas would not be sold or returned. In 1738, Spanish Florida promised land to runaway slaves. Therefore, slaves who migrated to Florida were provided some semblance of freedom by laws unavailable to slaves in other states. It is assumed that the great grandparent of Harry T. Moore originated from the Negroes in Florida who demonstrated tremendous bravery in the war between the Spanish and English; and therefore, won the right to be free before the Emancipation Proclamation of 1865.

Harry Tyson Moore was born November 18, 1905, of Johnny and Rosalea Moore, in Houston, Florida, a small farming town in the Panhandle of Suwannee County. It is certain that Moore's strong determination and unbreakable will to help his people were greatly influenced by his genetic makeup and his environmental exposure and guidance.

His father, plagued with illness, died in 1914 when Harry was only 9 years old. Due to the dangerous surroundings for a small Negro boy in a rural southern community, his mother sent Harry to live with her sister in Daytona Beach in 1915. In 1916, he was relocated to Jacksonville, Florida to live with his three highly educated and professional aunts, Jessie, Adrianna and Massie Tyson, two teachers and one nurse.

Harry was the only child in his maternal aunts' home. Under the watchful eye of his three loving aunties, he excelled at Florida Memorial High School receiving all A's and one B+ in French. After graduating from high school, he entered Bethune-Cookman College, founded by Mary McLeod Bethune, a strong Negro woman who was a world-renowned pioneer for a better quality of life for all people. Strongly influenced by Dr. Bethune, Moore received a Normal Degree from Bethune-Cookman in 1936 and immediately became an elementary school teacher in Cocoa, Florida.

During his early days in Cocoa, he learned the card game of bid whist and became quite skilled in playing the game. At one of the games, he met Harriette, a rather quiet, tall and beautiful female teacher. To fulfill a personal goal, Harry married Harriette Vyda Simms, who was born in Florida on June 19, 1902 making Harry three years Harriette's junior. The marriage was kept secret for several months because Harry's family had chosen another life mate for him.

Harry was promoted to the position of principal at the Titusville Colored School and Harriette soon joined him as one of his teachers. All in all, the marriage was a wonderful bond that produced two beautiful daughters, Annie Rosalea Moore (Peaches) born in 1928 and Juanita Evangeline Moore born two years later in 1930. This small family constellation, headed by the shy and quiet Harry T. Moore, would become the driving force that changed many patterns of injustice and discrimination against people of color in the state of Florida and in the world in general.

Home life at the Moores was truly a family affair. Harriette was often at her Singer Sewing machine making dresses with matching bloomers for the girls while Harry was helping them with homework. Dinner always included Harry's favorite cornbread and often fried chicken. Fresh vegetables from the garden complimented the evening meals. Because of a lingering stomach ailment, dinner took an hour or more since Harry was forced to eat very slowing. Dinner was never over until Harry finished eating. Because of the time that elapsed, his food had to be rewarmed by the girls during the meal. Often following the meal, Harriette played the piano in the living room to entertain the family. Other recreation included bid whist for the entire family at home and movies and/or restaurant meals in Sanford or Orlando because Harry refused to frequent the segregated facilities in Mims or Cocoa. The girls were transported by their father everywhere to avoid any harm from the ever-present Ku Klux Klan (KKK). Evangeline and Peaches observed frequent demonstrations of love and affection between Harry

12

and Harriette at home and in public. A close family bond prepared the family for the difficult challenges to come.

The imprint of genetics, a strong family bond and the influence of dedicated mentors left an enduring mark on Harry T. Moore's unwavering moral character and his courageous actions in quest of freedom for his people.

Our Children Must Learn About Their Culture and Be Responsible Citizens

Life as a student in a Harry T. Moore classroom was not the typical experience for Negro children in Florida. Most definitely, lessons in a Harry T. Moore classroom were quite different from the norm. Showing outstanding bravery, Moore departed from the required curriculum and brought from home journals and books depicting accomplishments of Negroes in the arts, medicine, politics and other fields. It was felt that knowledge of the successes of their people would motivate his students to excel. He emphasized the importance of participating in the political process long before the passage of the Voter Rights legislation in America. Moore was treading on very dangerous ground inasmuch as he would have certainly been fired for instilling in his students Negro pride and arming them with knowledge of how to use the political process to better their way of life. Because of the fearlessness of Moore, for the first time in Florida and perhaps in America, "*Negro History*" and civics were taught in public schools to Negro children.

In 1926 after Harriette joined Harry as one of his teachers in the Titusville Colored School, he purchased a Model T Ford in order for them to travel from Cocoa to Titusville, a very long four miles in those days. The Model T Ford proved to be an essential vehicle in years to come. While Principal, he supervised six teachers including his close friend John Gilbert who became a valuable support in the first fight for teacher equal rights in the white-dominated Deep South.

"Separate but equal" was the law of the land due to the *Plessy v. Ferguson* decision by the U. S. Supreme Court in 1896. Florida had its own special variety of "separate but equal", as Moore and his faculty witnessed; the 1885 Florida Constitution codified a most harsh version of "separate but equal":

- *illegal for Negro children and white children to be taught in the same schools*
- *illegal for Negro children to be taught by white teachers and white children to be taught by Negro teachers*
- *textbooks for white children were stored separately from textbooks for Negro children*

Before *Brown v. Board of Education*, Thurgood Marshall was Introduced to "Separate but Unequal" in Florida by Harry T. Moore

In addition to the Florida Constitution, the traditional patterns in Florida distinguished markedly the differences between the white public schools and the Negro public schools. The white school year comprised of nine months whereas the Negro school year was only eight months. The Negro students had second hand books that were worn books left over at the end of the white school year. Many schools with leaky roofs required Negro students to use umbrellas and raincoats during the school day. In rural Negro schools, indoor toilet facilities were nonexistent. The most egregious inequality existed in teachers' salaries. The Negro teachers throughout Florida received one half of the salaries of white teachers for the same positions. The basic salary for white teachers was $50.00 a month, with a unit value of $3.00 and a minimum salary of $100.00. For Negro teachers the basic salary was $20.00 a month, with a unit value of $2.00 and a minimum salary of $50.00. This inequity in teachers' salaries prompted Negro leaders to meet secretly under the guidance of Harry T. Moore and file the first lawsuit in the Deep South seeking equal teacher salaries across the races.

In 1937, five very brave Negro men held a secret meeting in Ocala that proved to be the impetus for the historic lawsuit for equalization of teacher pay in Florida. After much discussion; Harry T. Moore, principal of Titusville Colored School, Edward Davis, principal of Howard Academy and president of the Florida State

Teachers Association (FSTA), Noah W. Griffin, principal of

Gibbs High School, Dr. Gilbert Porter, principal of the

DeFuniak Springs High School and FSTA Attorney S. D.

McGill agreed to file the lawsuit in Brevard County. Each of

them risked their jobs and retributions from the KKK;

however, despite these fears, they continued with their

clandestine preparations.

At the request of Moore, John Gilbert stepped

forward and became the plaintiff in the Brevard County

lawsuit. This act cost Gilbert his job and resulted in his

seeking employment selling insurance. He never returned to

teaching. Although the filing in state court of the Gilbert

lawsuit proved to be the basis of its dismissal, similar

lawsuits bolstered by the pioneering efforts of Harry T.

Moore were successful in Federal court in the Florida

counties of Hillsborough, Palm Beach, Escambia, Duval, and

Dade.

Much of the success of the teacher equalization lawsuits was attributed to the skillful legal talents of Thurgood Marshall who was successfully recruited by Harry T. Moore to join their fight. Moore worked closely with Marshall during late night sessions at the Moore residence over a period of several years. Public hotel accommodations for Negroes were not available throughout the Deep South so private homes often filled the void before the Civil Rights Bill was passed. Eventually, all Florida counties equalized teachers' salaries for all races. The successful Florida lawsuits with Harry T. Moore leading the fight paved the way for much of the legal research in the 1954 ***Brown v. The Board of Education*** historical decision that changed public education in America forever.

During the time that Moore was fighting for equalization of teachers pay, he was very active in the NAACP, having founded the 1934 Brevard Chapter that focused on educational activities initially and eventually

Negro atrocities. Early activities in the Florida NAACP focused mostly on social festivities and celebrations that were the foundation of organizing local members. Moore was ever mindful of the dangers inherent in recruiting membership in a Negro-support group in the South. Because of the need to protect the members, social events were visible to the public at large and strategy meetings were held in secret.

The NAACP Becomes a Primary Focus for
Harry T. Moore

As predicted, organizers of the Gilbert lawsuit and other teacher equalization cases were targeted for dismissal by the state of Florida. Griffin and Davis were eventually fired with many other organizers of similar Florida lawsuits. Although she did not actively participate in the legal battles, Harriette was fired ([allegedly] "resigned" as reported in the record on June 6, 1946) with her husband Harry. The simultaneous firing of both parents left the Moore family with no viable source of income. Harry's organizing successes had gained him an enviable reputation that was recognized by the NAACP headquarter's leadership. Following his firing by the Brevard County School Board, on June 28, 1946 NAACP offered Harry a full-time job as an organizer with the title of Executive Secretary of the Florida NAACP Conference. This move was precedent setting since no other state had a paid position of NAACP Executive Secretary.

Life for Harry as a full-time NAACP organizer involved the full participation of the entire family. Although a brilliant speech writer, Harry was not so blessed with orator skills. He enlisted his youngest daughter Evangeline to deliver speeches at NAACP meetings and conventions. Evangeline, who was certainly a *"daddy's girl"*, reluctantly accepted the volunteer position and suffered frequent nightmares as she practiced the lengthy speeches that had to be given without notes of any kind. Eventually, she evolved into a very skilled public speaker and became well known for her outstanding delivery of her father's spirited speeches throughout the state. Evangeline also assumed leadership roles in the Florida NAACP Youth organization formed by her father.

During the time that Moore had pushed for the equalization of teachers' pay, he also involved the NAACP in other civil rights matters. The 1920's, 1930's and 1940's saw a flood of lynching in Alabama, Mississippi, Georgia and Florida. One of the most gruesome lynchings in the country was that of Claude Neal in 1934, the same year that the Brevard NAACP chapter was formed by Harry T. Moore. Following the rape and death of a white woman in Marianna, Florida, Neal was tortured and made to confess to the crime. He was mutilated by a white mob that forced him to eat his penis and testicles prior to killing him. The body was hung on the courthouse lawn. The National Guard had to be called to restore order. No one was ever convicted. The

NAACP campaigned vigorously to pass an antilynching bill without success in the aftermath of the Neal killing.

In 1943, two other Florida lynching cases thrust Harry T. Moore into action. Cellos Harrison was lynched in Marianna bringing back painful memories of the Neal murder in that town. Moore sent written pleas to the Governor to seeking justice in the senseless killing. The pleas did not result in any definitive action and no convictions followed. Shortly thereafter, a teenager, Willie James Howard, was killed in Florida for sending a Christmas card and an addition note to a white girl. To make matters worse, the teens' father was made to witness his murder. Again, no indictments or convictions were ever made. Moore enlisted the assistance of Thurgood Marshall who requested a full investigation by Federal authorities. Moore located the parents and took sworn affidavits that he sent to the Marshall for further investigation. Marshall sent the affidavits to the U.S. Attorney General who refused to enter the case citing the lack of jurisdiction. Investigations of many lynchings, bombings and burnings would be pursued by Moore who gained the reputation of being a "*trouble maker*"; and consequently, the target of many death threats to him and his family. Despite the intimidation, Moore continued to seek justice for victims in the Deep South with much vigor and resolve.

As Executive Secretary of the Florida NAACP Conference, his organizing campaigns and investigations of hate crimes perpetrated against Negroes took the family over the dangerous back roads of Florida during the evenings and weekends for several years. Moore worked diligently to establish NAACP chapters in the small rural towns plagued with KKK terrorism although the numbers of members recruited were much smaller than in the larger Florida cities. He crisscrossed the state to reach remote areas bringing the message of freedom and equality that would be possible with united determination. Moore's efforts resulted in an unbelievable 63 Florida NAACP branches at its height.

The Model T Ford became the transportation for the whole family in the struggle for equal rights and justice. Harriette and Harry would sit in the front seat with Harry at the wheel. The girls would sit in the back seat with toys, books and the ever-present lunch since no white restaurants would serve Negroes during their travels throughout the state.

The KKK made it their business to know the itinerary of Harry T. Moore, *"the negro agitator."* On many of his trips, he would be followed by Klansmen attempting to dissuade him from his mission with threats of violence. Evangeline's job was to look *"through the back window"* and report when she saw the lights of the cars following them turn on side roads indicating that they might be safe from immediate danger. In conversations with Evangeline, the author was told that she was unaware of the many threats on their life until she reached adulthood; and therefore, was not as fearful during the car rides.

Although much of Moore's efforts regarding killings and lynchings seemed to result in the same indifference of the entrenched "*good old boy*" system, an unexpected victory happened in 1945. The NAACP national journal, *Crisis*, reported that a colored boy accused of killing a white woman was taken to a death cell in Faiford, Florida and the sentence was commuted for further investigation with the assistance of the Florida NAACP branches.

Political Activity Takes Center Stage in
Harry T. Moore's Agenda

Since the beginning of his teaching career in Cocoa, Moore had encouraged school children to register and vote as a civic duty of every resident even before Negroes had the "*right to vote*" in Florida. To disenfranchise Negroes, Florida prohibited them from entering primary races. Local political authorities refused Negroes registration in the

Democratic Party which in effect eliminated them from any political influence since the elected officials in Florida were Democrats. Also, when Moore was teaching in Cocoa and served as Principal in Titusville, Florida had a two dollar poll tax. Negroes seeking voter registration frequently met with violence. Those who had the money and were brave enough to attempt registration could only register in the Republican Party. Despite those deplorable conditions in Florida, Moore gave his students sample ballots and held mock elections in the classroom. He openly challenged the Florida voting tradition that prohibited Negroes from participating in the primaries. During his struggles, he could not have predicted that his efforts would bear fruit as a result of the victory of his new ally--Thurgood Marshall.

In the spring of 1944, Thurgood Marshall won a U.S. Supreme Court case (*Smith v. Allwright*). allowing Negroes to enter into primary races--Texas's white primary law was ruled unconstitutional. Bolstered by this decision, Moore renewed his fight for Negroes to enter primary races and the Democratic Party. Following Reconstruction in both the north and south, most registered Negroes were Republicans, the party of Lincoln.

On August 31, 1944, Moore founded the Progressive Voters' League (PVL) with a mission to register Negroes and improve the voting climate in the state of Florida. The NAACP could not enter directly into such political activities because it had a nonpartisan charter that prohibited the nonprofit organization from endorsing candidates or encouraging registration in any specific political party. Moore saw the PVL as the answer to this dilemma and wholeheartedly embraced its objectives.

The first meeting of the PVL was held in Lake Wales, Florida. The main focus was a registration drive that enlisted the aid of churches, business leaders, and many organizations throughout the state. The PVL sought white sympathizers and included them among its membership. The successes of such unified efforts were immediately apparent when Negroes were allowed to register and vote freely as Democrats in Miami and Daytona Beach in 1945. Other Florida cities and town were much more resistant in allowing Negroes to register and/or vote as Democrats.

Moore himself was not allowed to register as a Democrat in his own Brevard County. He sent to Thurgood Marshall the circumstances surrounding the events that prevented him from changing his registration from Republican to Democrat. Marshall provided the information to the U.S. Attorney General for investigation. To stop any further erosion of the Democratic Party in Florida by the *"entrance of Negroes"*; in 1947, Florida Senator John E. Matthews of Jacksonville introduced the Matthews Bill to make the Democratic Party a private club that could determine its own membership. Moore immediately organized against the Matthews Bill and initiated a massive direct-mail campaign. The organized opposition resulted in the defeat of the Matthews Bill in the Florida Legislature. Eventually with pressure from the PVL, all Florida counties allowed Negroes to enter the political process, including voting in the Democratic primary, with only scattered bombings and infrequent killings in some KKK enclaves.

Moore clearly saw the relationship between political power and civil rights. He felt that Negroes could not substantially improve their situation without the power of the ballot. Empowered by the Matthews victory, he increased his teaching of Negroes to vote for sheriffs and other local and state officials who were more sympathetic to Negroes. Through the PVL, he developed papers presenting platforms of candidates. He wrote many candidates to ascertain their positions on specific issues that affected Negroes. Moore involved himself in numerous investigations where Negroes were refused voter registration privileges. He also studied each candidate's platform to determine the "best" choice for his people and rated candidates according to the level of support for views that improved the plight of Negroes.

Moore involved the PVL in local, state and Federal races. He endorsed candidates at all levels and encouraged the membership to vote in blocks to leverage their unified strength. Many letters were sent by Moore to the Florida Governor reporting activities that barred Negroes from registering and/or voting. Since these letters were largely ineffective in bringing about any immediate change, Moore began to write the U.S. Justice Department directly.

After extensive research by Moore, PVL endorsed Harry S. Truman for President in 1948 citing his (1) angry reactions to lynchings, (2) his executive order to eliminate segregation in the armed forces and (3) his appointment of the Committee on Civil Rights. PVL also endorsed several congressional candidates based on their responses to PVL surveys regarding civil rights issues. Because President Truman defeated Thomas Dewey by such a slim margin,

Negro voters in Florida began to see the political power of the ballot as Moore had been teaching all along. With the increase in the voting strength of Negroes, white southerners began to recognize the leadership of Moore in changing the southern traditions by elevating the political influence of the Negro. Because of this *"unwanted interference"*, Moore was once again labeled as a *"trouble maker."* The more radical elements began to suggest that something had to be done about Harry T. Moore.

One of the most important political defeats was attributed to the political prowess of Harry T. Moore in the spring of 1950. **A. Fortenberry (Fortenberry had no other first name than "*A*")** was a powerful Central Florida political machine who had been elected for many years as county commissioner. Fortenberry was also the Chairman of the Port Canaveral Authority. Several white businessmen drafted Dave Nisbet as a write-in challenger to Fortenberry because of their dissatisfaction with Fortenberry's alleged mismanagement of public funds. Moore met with Nisbet

and sought his views on issues affecting Negroes; and being

satisfied that he was the best candidate, recommended that

the PVL endorse Nisbet for county commissioner.

Fortenberry lost the election to the *"write in"* candidate

Nisbet because of the Negro vote. This election was hailed

as one of the biggest upsets in Central Florida history.

Moore gained sensational notoriety for his skillful tactics

that resulted in the Fortenberry defeat. White candidates

began to seek advice from Moore and requested the support

of the PVL during their campaigns.

Through the PVL, Moore encouraged Negroes to

register initially as Democrats or convert from Republicans

to Democrats. He endorsed specific Democratic candidates

who espoused PVL views on issue relevant to the Negro

community. Moore justified his urging Negroes to register as

Democrats by his statements in a letter to his NAACP

coworkers after explaining the increasing lynchings and

police brutality:

> *"Who controls the election of these state and county officials [referring primarily to sheriffs and other police officials], the Republicans or Democrats? Regardless to [sic] our party beliefs, we must now face facts. And the fact is that practically every city, county and state official in Florida is selected in the Democratic Primaries. In order to help select these officials, Negroes must vote in the Democratic Primaries. In order to vote in the Democratic Primaries, Negroes must register asDemocrats."*

Despite his logic, Republicans in the NAACP began

to complain about Moore's political activities in the PVL.

Moore's endorsements upset Republicans, both Negro and

white, many of whom provided financial support to the

NAACP. Also, Moore's habit of signing his letters and

position statements with both his NAACP and PVL positions

irritated the NAACP leadership. This practice prompted

some of the NAACP officials to request him to refrain from

the dual signatures on official correspondence. Moore's

refusal to do so eventually lead to unforeseen problems with

respect to his NAACP job.

Much of Moore's work with the NAACP and the PVL involved increasing the memberships of both organizations primarily in rural small communities and registering voters. Moore is credited with registering more than 116,000 voters in Florida, an unbelievable feat in the Deep South. Although Moore had accomplished establishing more chapters in a short period of time than any another state, NAACP officials urged him to concentrate more on increased membership in the larger cities that would bring more funds to the national headquarters. Not fully recognizing problems on the horizons, Moore continued his missions in both organizations with uncompromising zeal without changing his strategies or primary focus. In summary, Moore used his positions in both the NAACP and PVL to educate Negroes how to use their united powers to change long-standing traditions in the South for their betterment without considering the dangers to him and his family.

The problem with focusing on small community membership drives created a serious problem when the NAACP raised its annual dues from $1.00 to $2.00 in July, 1948. In spite of vehement opposition from Moore who complained that his poor membership could not afford the one dollar increase, the dues were increased to two dollars. The Florida membership plummeted causing a budget deficit and a significant loss of income for Moore's salary. The backlash from white southerners due to Moore's political victories, the problems of NAACP Republicans with Moore's using PVL to elect Democrats and Moore's concentration on small communities, put Moore in an unenviable position of opposition from both Negroes and whites.

Higher Education is an Equal Right for all Peoples

The battles to equalize teachers' pay in Florida did not extend itself to the right of Negro students to have equal access to educational facilities in the state of Florida or elsewhere in America. Moore took on the challenge to open higher education for Negroes in Florida with an initial appeal for a legal fund to pursue a lawsuit to open the University of Florida to Negroes. Several southern states, including Florida, paid "*scholarships*" for Negroes to attend out-of-state schools as a compromise for keeping their colleges and universities "*all white*." Moore contended that this practice was unacceptable and that all citizens of Florida should have equal access to state-funded institutions of higher education.

In December 1949, the lawsuit was heard before the Florida Supreme Court demanding that Negroes be admitted to the University of Florida. Virgil D. Hawkins was among the plaintiffs in the case as he had unsuccessfully sought admission to graduate and professional state-supported schools in Florida. Moore collaborated on the case with Attorney Alex Akerman, a white attorney who took the lead in many other Florida lawsuits seeking justice and equal treatment for Negroes in Florida. After a prolonged court battle, the case was decided favorably in 1958 with the admittance of Negro students to state-supported colleges and universities in the state of Florida.

The Rise in the Power of Southern Negroes was Accompanied by a Corresponding Rise in the KKK

As Negroes began to show political strength and Moore continued to investigate lynchings, burnings and bombings, the KKK increased their activities in many parts of Florida, urban and rural. One of the first incidents in the late 1940's occurred in Miami where two Negro homes were razed and a cross was burned at a nearby intersection following a fight between a Negro and white man. Cross burnings intended to intimidate Negroes from voting were reported frequently in Negro neighborhoods. In all of the investigations, sheriffs claimed that no suspects could be found. The Pittsburg Courier reported on the "arson wave" affecting Negro communities in Miami and cited that no arrests had been made.

An *"alleged"* crime took place in Lake County and involved one of the most famous rape cases in U.S. history.

On June 16, 1949 Norma Padgett had apparently been beaten by her husband who encouraged her to claim that she was raped to conceal his actions for fear of retribution from her family. When asked by the authorities who committed the crime, Norma implicated four Negro boys and said the boys assaulted her husband, abducted her in a car, raped her and left her on the side of the road on the outskirts of Groveland, Florida.

In 1949, Groveland was known as a KKK stronghold. Angry Klansmen entered Negro homes beat Negro men and boys and set many homes on fire indiscriminately after hearing of the alleged rape. Two returning Negro servicemen, who had refused to follow local law enforcement customs and refrain from wearing their U.S. Army uniforms in town, were targeted with two other Negroes from Groveland and accused of the alleged rape. Four hundred Negroes vacated the town as the homes burned during the mayhem, many never returned. The Florida Governor was forced to call in the National Guard to end the violence. Of the four suspects, Ernest Thomas eluded capture and was killed by a posse headed by Sheriff Willis McCall. The other suspects, Samuel Shepherd, Charles Greenlee and Walter Irvin, were arrested and allegedly transferred to another location *"for their safety."*

On July 20, 1949, Moore telegrammed Governor Warren: "*Florida branches of the NAACP urge prosecution of mob leaders responsible for terrorism and vandalism against innocent Negro citizens of Lake County.*" Moore also wrote the Florida State Attorney requesting an investigation of the mob violence adding that Sheriff McCall knew members of the mob and could easily arrest them for arson and mob violence.

Moore requested the legal assistance of the national NAACP. In response, the NAACP assembled a team of lawyers to defend the suspects and sent them to Florida. A change of venue was sought in view of the mob violence and the intimidation of Negroes in the immediate community, but the judge denied the request. All three suspects were quickly found guilty by the all-white jury. The judge announced a death sentence for Irvin and Shepherd and a life sentence for Greenlee, a minor at the time. A Groveland Defund Fund was established for an appeal. Thurgood Marshall was added to the appeal defense team. The first appeal was unsuccessful at the Florida Supreme Court level, but the U.S. Supreme Court overturned the convictions based on the hostile climate and adverse pretrial publicity. A new trial was ordered. Encouraged by the victory, Moore intensified his efforts to raise money for the Groveland Defense Fund.

Moore requested that Sheriff McCall be prohibited from guarding or escorting the prisoners based on accusations of brutal treatment of the suspects and his involvement in the killing of Thomas. Despite Moore's warning of potential harm to the suspects; on November 6, 1951, McCall set out to drive Shepherd and Irvin from the prison at Raiford to Tavares for a pretrial hearing. During the trip, McCall reported that he stopped to repair a tire and let the suspects out of the car to urinate. He further stated that he was forced to shoot both suspects when they attempted an escape notwithstanding the fact that they were handcuffed together. Shepherd died instantly and Irvin was seriously injured, although initially he was thought to have been killed at the scene. Miraculously, the critically wounded Irvin survived to tell reporters, Federal investigators and NAACP attorneys that McCall forced him and Shepherd out of the car and shot them in cold blood.

Following the killing, Moore immediately requested the suspension and arrest of McCall for the murder of the handcuffed suspects. Outrage gripped the nation and protests came from civic rights organizations, church groups, labor unions, and a myriad of other entities.   Hundreds of letters were sent to President Truman, the U.S. Attorney General and the Florida Governor protesting Shepherd's death and requesting a full investigation of the circumstances surrounding all aspects of the rape case and the death of Shepherd.

In addition to defending the Groveland suspects, one of the defense team members was tasked with investigating the Florida NAACP chapters while he was in Florida. It was rumored that the successes and popularity of Moore overshadowed the NAACP, and Moore's growing prominence was a problem for the headquarters office. A report was sent to the NAACP headquarters blaming Moore for the declining membership without any reference to the increase in dues that caused a financial hardship for Florida families.

After much dialogue between supporters and opponents, the decision was made to abolish the position of Executive Secretary of the Florida NAACP Conference. Moore was offered the unpaid position of Coordinator. Moore accepted the unsalaried position and maintained his activities of registering voters and investigating lynchings, bombings and other civil rights atrocities without any interruption. He continued to focus on seeking justice for the slain Shepherd calling for a Federal intervention in view of the hesitancy of local officials. To his disappointment, McCall was only investigated by local officials and was cleared of all charges by the Lake County Coroner. Because of the mounting death threats, Moore finally purchased a gun and kept it under his bed and in a bag in his car while he was traveling.

Prior to the Groveland incident, Harriette accepted a teaching position in Palm Beach that necessitated their moving to that area. Peaches had moved out of the home and Evangeline was in Washington, D.C. where she was working in the U.S. Department of Labor. With the daughters out of the house, Harry and Harriette closed their home in Mims and returned only for holidays and special occasions. Plans were made for the entire family and Harry's mother to celebrate Christmas together in Mims.

The Moores traveled from Palm Beach to Mims to attend their wedding anniversary party given in a close friend's home. Harry, Harriette, Peaches and Rosalea (Harry's mother) left the party and went to the Mims home about 9:00 pm Christmas night. Evangeline planned to travel to the homestead the day after Christmas as she was spending Christmas Day with her finances' family in the Nation's Capital. Nefarious events were underway that would change their lives forever.

Once at the Mims home, the four prepared for bed. Harry and Harriette shared fruitcake as a final anniversary act. Rosalea read the Bible for a while and afterwards went to bed in the back bedroom that had been added to the original house. Peaches read a book until she began to fall asleep. Harry aroused Peaches and encouraged her to go bed. Harriette went to bed after eating her fruitcake leaving Harry working in the living room. Soon after, Harry put away his work and joined Harriette in the same bed where they had shared their lives over the years. **BOOM!!!**

A bomb had been planted beneath Harry's and Harriette's bedroom at the right front of the house. It made such a large explosion that the living room furniture was hurled into the large crater made by the bomb. The bed fell on Harry and Harriette, making it difficult to see their bodies. The foundation of the house collapsed on the right corner. All of the windows in the house were shattered.

When the loud sound awakened Peaches, she ran down the short hall yelling and screaming at the top of her voice. Peaches opened her parents' damaged bedroom door and saw the large crater where her critically injured parents lay under the mass of rubble caused by the explosion. She screamed to her grandmother who witnessed the gruesome scene. Still screaming uncontrollably, Peaches ran outside and summoned her uncles George and Arnold Simms who lived a few yards away.

George and Arnold lifted the limp bodies from the crater. Harry and Harriette were carefully placed in George's car and transported some thirty-five miles away to the Fernald-Laughton Memorial Hospital in Sanford. They could not be taken to the nearest hospital in their community because Parrish Hospital did not admit Negroes. Also, the ambulance service in Titusville would not transport Negroes; consequently, a car without any emergency treatment available was the only transportation to the seriously injured Moores. Harry died on the way to the hospital and Harriette survived for a few days thereafter.

During the Christmas holidays, several meetings and barbeques were held where Klansmen discussed possible solutions to the "*Harry T. Moore problem*." It was rumored that one of the KKK meetings involved an interior drawing of the Mims house and the directions to travel there. Many southern sheriffs and other law enforcement officers were often members of the KKK. Even though there is no concrete evidence, it is assumed that Sheriff McCall was either a member of the KKK or would have KKK friends who would be very concerned about Moore's insistence that McCall be prosecuted for Shepherd's killing. Although the specifics of the KKK's backlash to Moore may never be known, it is fair to say that the KKK had a vested interest in silencing Harry T. Moore.

The assassination of Harry T. Moore and his wife made international news. Newspapers in many foreign countries carried the story as front page news. The Russian Ambassador to the United Nations charged the United States with not being able to protect its citizens and specifically violating the civil rights of Harry T. Moore. Interracial groups, civil rights organizations, churches, business leaders and many others urged immediate action leading to the arrest and conviction of the perpetrators. President Truman ordered an FBI investigation that would last several years. Despite hundreds of pages of FBI investigative reports, the crime was never solved. The FBI suspected the involvement of the KKK, but no charges followed. Much speculation pointed to

Sheriff McCall as financing the killings. On several occasions, the investigation was reopened, including the latest one in 2004 by Florida Attorney General Charlie Crist, again no convictions. Several local persons came forward suggesting their involvement or blaming others, but no definitive proof was ever found.

Harriette Chooses to Join Her Husband

Days before the funeral, Harriette was improving steadily, but she was troubled about the loss of her beloved Harry. Against the advice of her physician, Dr. George Starke the only Negro physician in Sanford, Harriette insisted on visiting her husband in the funeral home and having a final talk with him. Peaches and Evangeline took Harriette to Burton Funeral Parlor out of respect for their mother's wishes. No one knew what Harriette had in her heart as she made her way from the hospital to the Funeral Parlor.

Upon arriving at the Funeral Parlor, Harriette entered the room where her Harry was laying in his final resting encasement. She opened the casket and kissed her husband and began to whisper softly her last words to him. She turned toward her daughters and announced that she wished to be with her husband. Stunned, Evangeline asked her mother why she wanted to leave her and Peaches. Harriette, in a soft sincere voice explained that her life was now with her husband whom she had loved passionately from the first day she set eyes on him. She said that her job was done on earth as she and her husband had educated and raised two very fine daughters who have their own lives to live. Harriette returned to the hospital and went to heaven to join her husband on January 3, 1952, one day following Harry T. Moore's funeral.

The end

Epilogue

The following events have been influenced by the pioneering efforts of Harry T. Moore, the First Martyr of The Civil Rights Movement:

- 1952 award to Harry T, Moore the NAACP Spingarn Medal posthumously

- 1954 U.S. Supreme Court ***Brown v. Board of Education*** decision: ***"separate but equal"*** is unconstitutional

- 1955 U.S. Supreme Court decision: "school desegregation with all deliberate speed"

- 1964 Civil Rights Act

- 1965 Voting Rights Bill

- 1996 naming of the Harry T. Moore

  Justice Center in Cocoa

- 2004 establishment of the Harry T. and Harriette V. Moore Memorial Park and Museum

- 2006 reconstruction of the Moores' home by the state of Florida

- 2012 naming of the Harry T. and Harriette V. Moore Post Office in Cocoa

- 2013 designation of Florida Highway 46 for Harry T. and Harriett V. Moore

- 2013 induction into the Florida Civil Rights Hall of Fame

- 2014 making of the movie: *Before* SELMA...The Harry T. Moore Story

- 2015 recognition of Harry T. and Harriette V. Moore in the Smithsonian National Museum of African American History and Culture in Washington, D.C.

References and Notes

1. Cooper, Algia R., *"Brown v. The Board of Education and Virgil Darnell Hawking: Twenty-Eight Years and Six Petitions to Justice"*, Journal of Negro History 64 (Winter 1979), 1-20.

2. Crisis, National Association for the Advancement of Colored People. New York, 1935-53.

3. Florida Times-Union, 1950-52.

4. Green, Ben. Before His Time: The Untold Story of Harry T. Moore...America's First Civil Rights Martyr. Gainesville: University Press of Florida, 1999.

5. Harry T. Moore to F. Warren, Warren Papers, Series 235, Carton 53, Florida Archives

6. Harry T. Moore to J.W. Hunter, Warren Papers, Series 235, Carton 53, Florida Archives

7. Harry T. Moore to M. Caldwell, William Gray Papers. FAMU Negro Archives.

8. Interview by Dr. Florence Alexander with Evangeline Moore on April 12, 2012 at the Cocoa Beach Historical Society, Cocoa Beach, Florida.

9. Lawson, Steven, David Colburn and Darryl Paulson. *"Groveland: Florida's Little Scottsboro"*, Florida Historical Quarterly, 65, 1986.

10. <u>Miami Herald,</u> 1950-52.

11. <u>Miami Times,</u> 1950-52.

12. <u>New York Times,</u> 1950-52.

13. <u>Orlando Morning-Sentinel,</u> 1950-52.

14. Personal trips by Drs. Stanley and Florence Alexander to the Civil Rights Museums in Memphis, Tennessee and Chicago, Illinois.

15. Personal trip by Drs. Stanley and Florence Alexander to the original site of Fort Moses, St. Augustine, Florida, 2012.

16. Personal trips by Drs. Stanley and Florence Alexander to Senegal, Ghana and other African coastal regions during the 1990's and 2000's. During those many trips, the Alexanders experienced the very emotional feeling of going through the "Door of No Return" and viewing the ocean that lay beyond. After stepping on the rocks and sand outside the "Door", the Alexanders reversed their steps, went back into the slave castle through the "Door of Return" and continued their travels in Africa. For Harry T. Moore's forbearers, there was no "Door of Return" for they were not allowed to reenter the "Door" and return to their homeland. Instead, they entered the awaiting slave ship and set sail to unfamiliar lands in the Carribeans and Americas.

17. <u>Pittsburg Courier,</u> 1944-52.

18. Conversations with Jaunita Evangeline Moore.
2013-2014,

Acknowledgments

I wish to express my sincere appreciation to Jaunita Evangeline Moore for her generosity in sharing with me her knowledge and experiences while living with her father during his pioneering activities in the Civil Rights Movement. Without the endorsement of **"Daddy's Girl"** who was the lookout **"through the back window"**, this project would not have been possible. The pictures in this book were provided by Jaunita Evangeline Moore.

My immediate family played a vital role in helping me to gain insights into the characters of the subjects and to assemble much of the research involved in the writing of this book. Dr. Stanley Alexander, my loving husband, was always at my side and provided valuable financial support during the many trips to Africa, Fort Moses, Titusville, Florida, and the various Civil Rights Museums in the country. My son, Nathan Arthur Hicks, III drove me to the Harry T. and Harriette V. Moore Cultural Complex in Mims,

Florida and spent many hours copying hundreds of newspaper articles, magazine articles, letters, manuscripts and other materials used in the research of this book.

The encouragement of William (Bill) Gary, President of the Harry T. and Harriette V. Moore Cultural Complex Inc. Board was a constant inspiration for me to continue researching the life of this great unsung hero. I am very grateful for his steadfast dedication and leadership role in this project. I wish to thank the Harry T. and Harriette V. Moore Board members for their assistance in providing me with some of the more personal aspects of the story. I thank the Harry T. and Harriette V. Moore Memorial Park and Museum staff for their assistance. I especially appreciate Jaunita Barton who was very kind to me and provided the much-needed guidance in helping me locate materials in the Museum.

Friends and associates are appreciated for the role they played in my writing of this book. Milton Howard provided a wonderful cover that depicts the story in a very graphical way. Victor Scott is appreciated for taking professional photographs of the pictures and artifacts that are displayed in the Harry T. and Harriette V. Moore Museum in Mims, Florida. Valuable time was gained by having in my home office the photographic images of various events and subjects displayed in the Museum. Kenneth Winslow drove me to the Harry T. and Harriette V. Moore Board meetings located at the site of the reconstructed home and the Museum where I was able to walk on the grounds and personally experience the surroundings where significant events of the story took place.

A Special thanks is given to my Creator who gave me my devoted parents, Octavia and McKinley Johnson, both college graduates in the fields of chemistry and physics in the mid 1930's. Failing to obtain work at the local chemical plant because of their race, they both became teachers in all-Negro southern schools and experienced many of the trials and tribulations of Harry T. Moore and his wife. They lived to tell their daughter about the racist climate in America during the Jim Crow years and the many obstacles they overcame with perseverance and courage. Their devotion to me and their words: "You can be anything you want to be, all you have to do is prepare yourself" has sustained me during the darkest years of my life.

This book has truly been a labor of love since some events in my life paralleled that of the Moore family. I wish to thank my mother, who is now in heaven, for taking me on trips through Virginia in the 1940's. I remember stopping in restaurants that refused to allow me to use the restroom facilities forcing me to go outside in the field—this gave me personal insight into my conversations with Evangeline who also could not use restroom facilities in Florida because of her race. I wish to thank my father for shielding me from harm when I left my shotgun house by escorting me in my southern community just as Harry T. Moore did for his daughters. A piano played by my mother in our living room was the main source of music for the family because concerts and other musical events were closed to Negroes where I spent my early years in Appomattox, Virginia where I was born and Charleston, West Virginia during my primary and secondary school years. My parents always prepared lunches to take with us during car trips through the South just as the Moores did for their girls because of the lack of public accommodations for Negroes. Mother insisted that I be a "straight A" student making me ever mindful that a Negro in America needed a superior education to overcome the challenges that lay ahead. For my wardrobe prior to entering West Virginia State College, mother made me several new skirts and a winter coat on her manual Singer Sewing machine. Much of the experiences in writing this book took me back to my childhood and early adult days growing up in the South, and with this sensitivity I have a unique understanding of and appreciation for the "The Harry T. Moore Story."

I am truly grateful for the love of parents who have always been an inspiration for me to give back through educational pursuits and the sharing of my writings.

About the Author

 Dr. Florence Alexander is President of Ebon Research Systems, LLC, a management consultant firm she started in 1970. Following her two years at West Virginia State College (a land grant Historical Black College and University (HBCU), she transferred to The Ohio State University where she received a Bachelor of Science in Nursing. Her Master of Science Degree was awarded in the areas of Administration and Nursing from the Catholic University. She received a Ph.D. from the University of Maryland in the fields of Human Development Education, Research and Evaluation. Her academic achievements were recognized with top honors from her Alma Matas.

Dr. Alexander began her business career in the basement of her home with only a manual typewriter while a single mom rearing her young son. Overcoming many hurdles of racism, sexism and "bullying", she drew on her inner strength and internalized a standard of excellence in reaching seemingly impossible goals. Ebon Research Systems employed in excess of 1,200 full-time staff and grossed more than $417 million dollars in sales in its first twenty-four years. Dr. Alexander's entrepreneurial journey has taken her into the minefields of Federal government contracting and through the challenging terrain of pursuing education. During her formative years, Florence experienced separate facilities for whites and Negroes, similar to the Moores. From the first to the twelfth grades, she used second hand books in segregated schools. Seeking a terminal degree, she recalls that upon entering the University of Maryland her Major Professor and Head of the Department said to her: "I do not believe in women in higher education." She responded: "This is a new experience for me; I am so accustomed to being discriminated against because I am black, I am sure I can handle sexism." Dr. Alexander lived to witness that same professor tell the University of Maryland Dissertation Review Committee comprised of 15 white Ph.D.'s: "This is the finest dissertation I have had the pleasure of evaluating during my many years at the University of Maryland." To give back to society, she and her husband founded the Ebon International Preparatory Academy with 17 buildings on 44 acres in Forsyth, Georgia for disenfranchised youth.

Dr. Alexander is an accomplished author. One of her earlier published books, *Blacks in the Westward Movement,* was written for a Federal contract awarded to her firm Ebon Research
Systems by the Smithsonian Institution in 1974. The book was an integral part of a Smithsonian Institution traveling museum project featuring contributions of Blacks in America. She authored *Women in the Army...Improved Race Relations in the U.S. Army: Baseline Information on Minority Careers and Racial Harmony in the United States* and the *Study of the Advisory Committees for the U.S. Commission on Civil Rights* for the Federal government. Among her books written about historical figures are: *A Woman Who Dared to Be Somebody* and *Dare to Be A Success Business Woman Who Beat the Odds* (autobiographies of Dr. Florence Alexander), *Mary McLeod Bethune, Her Own Works of Inspirations* and the following biographical children's books written in English and Spanish: *Martin Luther King, Jr., Roberto Clemente, Cesar Chavez* and *Mary McLeod Bethune.* Her children's

books were converted into talking books so they would accessible to the blind. Her health-related books and papers include: ***Health Policy and Planning in the Urban Community, National Health Care Crisis: Its Impact in the District of Columbia and Possible Solutions, The Three A's Authorization, Allocation and Appropriation Regarding Sickle Cell Disease Federal Funding, Training Neighborhood Health Aides*** and ***Variables Associated with the Participation of a Group of Nonwhite Mothers in a Selected Health Department Birth Control Program.***

She has been received more than 50 awards including the Federal Woman's Award, the Martin Luther King, Jr. Drug Major for Justice, Entrepreneur of the Year, Kennedy Space Center Small Business of the Year, Who's Who International, Madame C. J. Walker Award, Atlanta Business League Woman of the Year, National 4-H Award, Toastmasters International Communications Leadership Award, SBA Minority-woman Owned Business of the Year and the Distinguished Alumnus from The Ohio State University.

Dr. Alexander was the first African American to serve as a Florida Elector. She is a charter member of the Senatorial Inner Circle.

Her community and professional activities are numerous. Dr. Alexander serves on the Harry T. and Harriette V. Moore Board in Mims, Florida. She is a life member of the NAACP, National Urban League, Alpha Kappa Alpha Sorority, and National Council of Negro Women. She is a Board member of the National Congress of Negro Women founded by U.S. Representative Shirley Chisholm. Past and present memberships include: American Educational Research Association, American Nurses Association, American Public Health Association, Business and

Professional Women's Club and various Chambers of Commerce.

Her immediate family includes her husband, Dr. Stanley Alexander, daughter Michelle Alexander, M.D., and two sons: Nathan Arthur Hicks, III and Stanley Alexander Jr. She has seven grandchildren.

APPENDIX

The Christmas 1951 Murders of
Harry T. and Harriette V. Moore

Results of the Attorney General's Investigation
Charlie Crist, Attorney General*

EXECUTIVE SUMMARY

I. Introduction

On Christmas Night, 1951, a bomb exploded under the bedroom of Harry T. and Harriette V. Moore's home in Mims, Florida. The couple had gone to bed after celebrating both Christmas and their 25th wedding anniversary. Mr. Moore was killed in the blast; Mrs. Moore died nine days later. One of the couple's daughters, Annie Rosalea, was at home but uninjured in the explosion. Their other daughter, Evangeline, was en route to Mims by train when the bomb exploded.

This murder silenced one of Florida's civil rights pioneers, and, while the term was not used frequently in 1951, there can be no question that it was carried out by 1950s-style domestic terrorists. For more than 50 years, the Moores' direct and extended family, their friends, and those interested in justice have hoped for resolution or solid evidence that would identify those responsible for such a cowardly act of violence. This is especially true of the Moores' surviving daughter, Evangeline, who has never lost that hope.

Prior to the Attorney General's decision to reopen the case, three prior investigations by federal, state and local law enforcement agencies sought to uncover what happened, why, and who was involved. Despite uncovering important information about the bombing, no arrests were ever made. By reviewing the results of prior investigations and by obtaining new information during the course of this investigation, the Attorney General believes that at least four of those responsible for committing or conspiring in the murders have been identified.

II. Who Were Harry and Harriette Moore?

Harry T. Moore and his wife Harriette were educators by profession. They lived in Mims, Florida, a small citrus town near Orlando, and they taught in the segregated public schools in and around Brevard County from 1925-46. Harry became principal of the Titusville Colored School in 1927. In addition to his work as an educator, Harry tended the orange groves around Mims.

---

*   The Attorney General's Office gratefully acknowledges the assistance of many interested individuals including author Ben Green, who generously shared his time and research; Bill Gary, President of the Brevard Chapter of the NAACP and numerous other NAACP officials; author Gary Corsair, whose book, *The Groveland Four*, provided valuable insight on race relations at the time; and Juanita Barton, director of the Moore Cultural Center, who graciously shared her time, information and coffee with investigators during their time in Mims. Finally, the Attorney General's Office commends the hard work and dedication put in to this investigation by FDLE Special Agent Supervisor Dennis Norred and Office of Civil Rights Investigator Frank Beisler.

1

The Moores were a quiet couple and spent their leisure time with family, particularly their two daughters. There was no evidence of any marital strife. They enjoyed reading, playing cards (particularly bid whist) and occasionally went to movies in Daytona Beach.

Harry became active in the early stages of the civil rights movement in the 1930s. He formed the Brevard County NAACP in 1934 and served as the NAACP's first statewide Executive Secretary. The focuses of his efforts were varied. He fought against lynchings, police brutality and inequities in the criminal justice system. He fought for equality in teacher salaries in Florida's segregated schools, the ability of blacks to vote in primary elections, and the registration of more black voters in the Democrat Party.[1]

Harry Moore's activities did not win him friends among those who wished to retain the status quo. The teaching contracts of Harry and Harriette Moore were not renewed in 1946. In 1951, the Moores were spending much of their time at a residence in South Florida and visited their Mims residence for occasional visits, especially during holidays.

III. Why Were The Moores Killed?

Over the years, a number of motives have been suggested for the Moores' murders. All of them share a common theme - retribution against Harry Moore for his civil rights activities. Especially challenging to the investigations has been sorting through the various rumors surrounding the murders, including rumors that local and state officials knew of or covered up the crime. In the interests of completeness, the following is a brief discussion of the various motives that have been suggested to the investigators looking at this case over the years. No evidence, however, has linked anyone to the murders other than the four members of the Ku Klux Klan identified in this report. It is, of course, possible that additional individuals were involved in the bombing.

(a) The Ku Klux Klan

The Ku Klux Klan was highly active in Florida during this period, including areas near Mims such as Lake County, Apopka and Orlando. The various investigations indicate that Harry Moore's name was a topic of discussion during some Klan meetings. It was generally believed that high ranking members of the communities, including law enforcement officers, elected officials, and prominent business owners, were members of the Klan or shared its beliefs.

(b) The Groveland Incident

In 1949, four black men (known as the Groveland Four) were accused and convicted of raping a white woman in Lake County, Florida. In 1951, the United States Supreme Court overturned their convictions. Lake County Sheriff Willis McCall, claiming that he acted in self-defense, killed two of the defendants as they were riding in the back of his car on their way to Lake County for their retrial. Moore began an active and prominent campaign against Sheriff McCall, including calling for his indictment in letters to Governor Fuller Warren and federal officials. While it appears that Moore's activities angered local and state officials, as well as members of the Klan, there is no evidence linking the Moore bombing to the Groveland case or Sheriff McCall.

---

[1]   In keeping with the 'Jim Crow' laws in effect through much of the South at that time, Florida engaged in the systematic exclusion of blacks from primary and general elections, a practice subsequently struck down by the United States Supreme Court.

2

(c) Local Political Activities

In addition to his voter registration activities, Moore and colleagues from the Brevard County NAACP formed the Progressive Voters League (PVL). The PVL became active in local and state elections. In the 1950 election for chairman of the Brevard County Commission, Moore endorsed a write-in candidate, David Nisbet, over the incumbent, Andrew Fortenberry. When Nisbet won, political observers attributed it to the black vote and Moore's activities. Although Fortenberry was bitter about his defeat and blamed Moore, no evidence links him to the bombing.

Moore also became involved in attempts to improve teachers' salaries and facilities at the local, segregated schools. His activism cost both himself and his wife their jobs in 1946 when their teaching contracts were not renewed, and the FBI investigated local school board officials after the bombing. No evidence, however, links them to the bombing.

(d) The NAACP

Moore's political activities did not meet with the approval of everyone in the NAACP, and some board members felt he was not spending sufficient time tending to the affairs of the Association as Executive Secretary. Less than one month before he was murdered, the Board voted to remove him as Executive Secretary. Some witnesses believed that someone close to the Moores might have been involved but no evidence linked anyone close to them, or within the black community, to the crime.

IV. Previous Investigations

As noted above, there have been three prior investigations of the Moore bombing. The original investigation by the Federal Bureau of Investigation (FBI) began immediately after the bombings and remained active until 1955. Hundreds of interviews were conducted in five states, while surveillance and informants were used to bolster any physical evidence. Two primary suspects were identified, but both died of natural causes before any charges were filed.

In 1978, the Brevard County State Attorney and Brevard County Sheriff reopened the case at the request of officials from the National Association for the Advancement of Colored People (NAACP). Results of the original FBI investigation were thoroughly reviewed and the role of a possible suspect was enhanced by the revelations of a dying individual whose story passed important tests for credibility.

In 1991, Governor Lawton Chiles ordered the Florida Department of Law Enforcement (FDLE) to investigate new information provided by a woman who claimed that her ex-husband was present at the bombings. No evidence was discovered that substantiated her claims.

A. The FBI Investigation: 1951-1955

The FBI immediately began an investigation following the Moores' murders. This four-year investigation involved at least 78 Special Agents who conducted over 1,000 interviews in Florida, Georgia, North Carolina, South Carolina and California. Investigative strategies also included telephone surveillance, confidential informants – many of whom were members of the Klan – and laboratory analysis of physical evidence gathered from the scene. Agents focused on developing background information on the Moores, particularly Harry's activities leading up to his death, as well as possible motives for the murders.

3

This was a difficult investigation, complicated by the black community's distrust of law enforcement. As a result, it is likely that some witnesses were not completely candid with investigators, while others feared retaliation by an active Klan.

Establishing federal jurisdiction presented another difficulty. The FBI did not normally investigate local murders, but Harry Moore had become a local hero in the black community and a nuisance to some politicians. His murder made national headlines, and it was feared that racial tensions throughout the country would mount if the case was not solved. Local officials were ill equipped to handle the case with their limited resources, and an FBI civil rights investigation was therefore opened even though the real issue was murder.

The FBI developed a number of primary suspects. In the weeks after the bombing, confidential informants led FBI agents to Earl J. Brooklyn and Tillman H. Belvin. Both were renegade Klansmen who had been expelled from another Klavern for being too violent. One informant claimed that Brooklyn had displayed a floor plan of the Moores' home at a Klan meeting about a year before the bombings. Another informant has asked Belvin early in 1952 if he had any dynamite, to which Belvin replied "No, I used it all on the last job."

According to the FBI, various Klansmen they were investigating began implicating other Klansmen in participating in other acts of Klan-sponsored violence, but could not provide admissible evidence in order to bring them to trial. Since these Klan informants could not be prosecuted for state crimes to which they were confessing – such as the bombing of an Orlando ice cream parlor and various beatings – the FBI decided to seek indictments against some for perjury in order to place more pressure to provide admissible evidence.[2] A federal grand jury returned indictments for perjury in June, 1953 but all were quashed by January, 1954 for lack of federal jurisdiction. The FBI closed its investigation in 1955.

Belvin died of natural causes in August, 1952 and Brooklyn died of natural causes on Christmas Day, 1952, exactly one year after the bombings.

B. Brevard County Sheriff and State Attorney's Investigation: 1978

The Brevard County Sheriff's and the State Attorney's Offices reopened the Moore case in 1978 at the request of the NAACP. Sheriff Rollin Zimmerman assigned Captain Winton J. Patterson to the case. Patterson uncovered important information when he was contacted by Edward Lee Spivey, a former high-ranking Klansman, as a result of the publicity surrounding the investigation. Spivey, who was dying of cancer, told Patterson that he knew who did the bombing and wanted to clear his conscience.

Spivey implicated his good friend and fellow Klansman Joseph Cox. Cox had been interviewed by the FBI during its investigation. Spivey claimed that Cox came to him the day after his second FBI interview and confessed that he "had done something wrong." According to Spivey, Cox said that he had been paid $5,000 to plant the bomb and had used the money to pay off the mortgage on his house. Cox was concerned that the FBI would find out about the mortgage payment and trace the crimes to him. Cox then borrowed Spivey's shotgun, went home and committed suicide.

---

[2] During their interviews with FBI agents, many of the Klan informants had lied about their involvement in the Klan and various Klan activities.

4

Transcripts of the tape recordings of Spivey's meetings with the investigators also reveal Spivey's bigotry and concern for the Klan's reputation because the bombings were not officially authorized. Spivey repeatedly notes that Cox's actions were not sanctioned by the Klan – a fact Spivey would know due to his position of "Exalted Cyclops" at the time.

FBI records and Cox's death certificate confirm that he had, in fact, committed suicide the day after his second FBI interrogation. Patterson and Assistant State Attorney Joel Dick presented this information to then-State Attorney Douglas Cheshire with a recommendation to prepare the case for grand jury presentment. Cheshire was said to be interested, but later lost his bid for reelection. Patterson and Dick were reassigned to other matters and the case was closed. Spivey died in August, 1980.

C. Florida Department of Law Enforcement Investigation: 1991

On August 30, 1991, Governor Lawton Chiles directed the FDLE to investigate information received from author Stetson Kennedy.[3] According to Kennedy, Orlando resident Dorothy Harrington indicated that her former husband, Frank Harrington, told her on at least six to eight occasions that he was present at the time of the Moore bombing.

FDLE Inspector John Doughtie was placed in charge of the investigation. He interviewed Ms. Harrington who related the story concerning her husband. Frank Harrington was interviewed a few weeks later. Frank admitted to being a member of the Klan in the late 50s or early 60s, a few years after the Moore bombings, but denied any knowledge of or participation in the Moore bombing. Frank later took and passed a polygraph examination.[4] Although Dorothy Harrington agreed to take a polygraph examination, it was never administered. Doughtie reviewed the results of previous investigations, interviewed family members and others who might have some knowledge of Harrington's activities. None of the documents or interviews revealed any information to contradict or support Frank or Dorothy Harrington's testimony.

The FDLE also examined the validity of a 1978 confession from Raymond Henry, a previous suspect in the FBI investigation. In his confession, Henry claimed that he was hired to make the bomb and carry out the crime, and also identified four other individuals as involved. Members of the FDLE interviewed Henry twice. During these interviews, he essentially recanted his 1978 confession, admitting it was a lie based on rumor, speculation and hearsay. Independent sources confirmed that much of the information provided by Henry in 1978 was not credible.

Finally, the FDLE researched the rumors concerning the possible involvement of Sheriff McCall, as well as a group of Klansmen known as the "Sydney Walker Hopper Group," in the Moore murders. No evidence was obtained that would link either McCall or the "Sydney Walker Hopper Group" to the crimes.

The FDLE's March 24, 1992 Investigative Summary indicated that the FDLE was unable to prove Ms. Harrington's claims and firmly discredited Raymond Henry's "confession."

---

[3]   Kennedy is the author of several books and articles concerning the Klan.
[4]   The Attorney General's Office interviewed Michael Mann, the FDLE Agent who administered the test to Frank Harrington. Mann recalled Harrington's exam and said that, while Harrington did express negative feelings towards African-Americans, he was telling the truth about his lack of involvement or knowledge of the Moore bombing.

V. The Attorney General's Investigation

On December 21, 2004 Attorney General Charlie Crist announced that the Moore case would be reopened and investigated through the Attorney General's Office of Civil Rights. The purpose was to review the history of the case and previous investigations and to seek any new witnesses or information that could lead to the identity of those responsible.

With the assistance of the FDLE, a team of experienced investigators and attorneys began an intensive, 20-month investigation into this case. It was the most comprehensive review ever performed of this case, and included a thorough examination of the information gathered in the prior investigations, a quest for new information, interviews of more than 100 people, and a complete excavation of the bomb site. The team spent thousands of hours in the field interviewing witnesses, gathering and examining physical evidence, writing notes and reports and following investigative leads.

Much of the team's research focused on a series of bombings which occurred in Florida a few months before the Moore bombing. Those bombings were believed to have been set by members of the Ku Klux Klan operating in Florida. During the FBI's investigation, agents interviewed a number of Klan members concerning these incidents to gain information on the Klan and the Moore bombing. As noted above, the FBI charged some of the Klansmen with perjury, and those proceedings were extensively reviewed by the team to gather background, potential witnesses for examination and investigative leads. Although the FBI's investigation was extensive, the team located and interviewed area residents and suspected Klan members who were not previously interviewed.

The team also examined other civil rights cases which have been reopened and solved in recent years. These were important guides in going forward with this investigation, although they ultimately enjoyed dramatic evidentiary breakthroughs not found here. For example, in some of those cases, the perpetrators were identified by evidence available in the initial investigation but suppressed or ignored at the time. In other cases, new witness statements or analyses of physical evidence identified the criminals.

The Office was fortunate to obtain valuable assistance from the Florida Association of Crime Stoppers, who posted a $25,000 reward to prompt people with new information to come forward. The group also produced an extensive media campaign using radio and television advertisements and billboards to heighten public awareness of the investigation. New discoveries about the crime were obtained from tips generated through Crime Stoppers.

No physical evidence was available to examine due to its loss or destruction. The FBI advised the team it had returned most of the evidence in its possession to the Brevard County Sheriff's office following their original investigation. By the time of this investigation, those items had long since been destroyed. Investigators questioned witnesses regarding whether they had taken any items from the site following the bombing as people often do given the historical significance of the murders. Witnesses were also asked if they knew anyone who claimed to have any artifacts from the bombing. Some items of personal property and debris from the bombing are displayed at the Moore Cultural Center in Mims, Florida. These items were transported by investigators to the FBI Laboratory in Quantico, Virginia on August 25, 2005. Laboratory tests conducted using the latest in research and investigative techniques did not reveal any new information concerning the crimes.

6

In an effort to discover any existing artifacts, the bomb site was excavated by archeologist Thomas Penders and Associates on December 2, 2005. While the FBI conducted a limited excavation, this was the most comprehensive and professional excavation of the site ever conducted. Archeologists verified the location of the Moore house and site of the explosion. More than one hundred bags of artifacts were recovered and forwarded to FBI laboratory in Quantico, Virginia for analysis. Those tests, however, did not produce any evidence of significance to the case.

All available evidence - physical, testimonial, and documentary – suggests dynamite as the explosive most likely used. It was readily available and many people - including all of the primary suspects - were familiar with its usage from working in the orange groves.

Finally, the team pursued an investigation of any evidence linking the principal suspects to monies paid for the murders. This included title searches of properties owned by the principal suspects, as well as a search of relevant financial records, in an effort to determine whether recorded transactions coincided with the general timeframe of the murders.

Despite being hampered by the passage of time, the destruction of physical evidence and the death of key witnesses, the team was able to discover new information that bolsters some of the previous conclusions about the case and provide new information on how the bombings were carried out and who was involved.

VI. The Suspects

This investigation points to the probable involvement of four individuals: Earl Brooklyn, Tillman Belvin, Joseph Cox and Edward Spivey. All had a long history of Klan involvement, and Brooklyn, Belvin and Cox were former members of the Association of Georgia Klan. They later joined the Orlando Klan and, along with Spivey, served as officers of that Klavern. Brooklyn, Belvin and Spivey all served a tenure as "Exalted Cyclops" and Cox served as the Secretary. Brooklyn and Belvin were considered renegade Klansmen because their attack methods were often contrary to Klan policies. They were reportedly trying to recruit others to go with them to the Moores' house. Cox, who was running for office, had a strong motive to get involved since Moore had demonstrated his effectiveness at influencing elections.

Previous investigations were crucial to putting these pieces together. The FBI's investigation identified two of the suspects – Brooklyn and Belvin. Both suspects died of natural causes within one year of the bombing and no charges were brought prior to their deaths. As summarized above, statements made by both Brooklyn and Belvin implicated them in the murders.

Title searches conducted during this investigation tend to bolster a connection between Belvin and the murders. Belvin purchased property in 1946 for $5,000 under terms that called for satisfying the mortgage in 1953. That mortgage was satisfied on December 21, 1951 – four days before the bombing. It must be noted, however, that Belvin re-mortgaged the property in February, 1952 for $5,000. Nine days after the bombing he sold a separate piece of property that he owned free and clear and purchased additional property in February, 1952.

The FBI interviewed Cox twice, and he committed suicide following the second interview in 1952. Cox did not emerge as a suspect, however, until the 1978 investigation by the Brevard County Sheriff's Office, when investigators were advised of his possible culpability by his friend Spivey. Contrary to Spivey's statement regarding Cox's payment for the bombings, however, a

7

search of county and bank records did not produce documentation of a satisfied mortgage for Cox at the time of the bombing.[6]

Based on information provided to this investigation by the 1978 investigators, this investigation has also concluded that - given the consistency with which Spivey retold the story of Cox's involvement and Spivey's detailed knowledge of the Moores' house on the night of the bombing[6] - Spivey may have had some involvement in the planning or execution of the crime. Spivey met six to eight times with Captain Winton Patterson, the lead investigator assigned to the 1978 investigation. Captain Patterson told this team that during each meeting Spivey's story was remarkably consistent and full of vivid detail, despite Spivey's ill health and drinking problem. At Captain Patterson's request, Assistant State Attorney Joel Dick, the chief homicide prosecutor for the Brevard State Attorney's Office at the time, accompanied Patterson to a meeting with Spivey. Captain Patterson wanted ASA Dick, an experienced prosecutor, to see Spivey and evaluate his credibility. Dick told this investigation that, after meeting Spivey and hearing his information, Dick had concluded that Spivey was telling the truth about Cox and also suspected Spivey may have had a role in the bombing because of his detailed knowledge.[7]

VII. Conclusion

Available evidence, although not conclusive, links Belvin, Brooklyn, Cox and, to a lesser extent, Spivey, to the crimes. While the evidence is not conclusive, it is very strong. It is the opinion of those involved in this investigation that, were any of these suspects still alive, sufficient circumstantial evidence exists to present the case to a grand jury for possible indictments for the Moores' murders.

It is also possible that other members of the Klan, especially the Orlando and Apopka Klaverns, participated in the conspiracy to murder the Moores. The record shows Moore and his activities were discussed at several Klan meetings and members were not pleased with Moore's growing success at changing the existing political structure. While the murders may not have been officially sanctioned by the Klan and the perpetrators were considered "renegades," other members of the Klan definitely knew Moore was being targeted.

It is also sadly evident that some members of area law enforcement were Klan members and/or sympathizers and may not have supported the FBI's investigation. The damage caused by that regrettable state of affairs is still evident today, as this investigation concluded that a number of witnesses were reluctant to be completely candid with this investigation for fear of retribution.

---

[6]   In 1946, five years before the bombing, he acquired three additional parcels of land, expanding the total acreage of his homestead. These additional parcels were acquired at a tax sell without a mortgage. Therefore, there was no record of a mortgage for any part of Cox's homestead at the time of the bombing.

[6]   Details revealed by Spivey over twenty-five years after the murders included that the shades were down and the windows to the Moores' house were closed, that Cox had to crawl under the house to plant the bomb, and that Christmas music could be heard from outside the house and the Christmas tree was visible from the woods.

[7]   A search of property and other financial records relating to Spivey did not provide any additional evidence to bolster this conclusion. A little search on Spivey's property revealed that he re-mortgaged his house several times to satisfy IRS tax liens and private judgments. One such re-mortgage was satisfied in January, 1951, too far in time from the bombing to reasonably infer a connection between the two

8

Congressional Record
112th Congress
(2011-2012)

HARRY T. AND HARRIETTE MOORE POST OFFICE
(House of Representatives - November 28, 2012)

[Page: H6482]
Mr. GOSAR. Mr. Speaker, I move to suspend the rules
and pass the bill (H.R. 2338)
to designate the facility of the United States Postal
Service located at 600 Florida
Avenue in Cocoa, Florida, as the ``Harry T. and
Harriette Moore Post Office''.
The Clerk read the title of the bill.

The text of the bill is as follows:

H.R. 2338
*Be it enacted by the Senate and House of
Representatives of the United States of
America in Congress assembled,*

SECTION 1. HARRY T. AND HARRIETTE MOORE
POST OFFICE.

(a) *Designation*.--The facility of the United States Postal
Service located at 600
Florida Avenue in Cocoa, Florida, shall be known and
designated as the ``Harry T. and
Harriette Moore Post Office''.

(b) *References*.--Any reference in a law, map,
regulation, document, paper, or other record of the
United States to the facility referred to in subsection

(a) shall be deemed to be a reference to the ``Harry T. and Harriette Moore Post Office''.

The SPEAKER pro tempore. Pursuant to the rule, the gentleman from Arizona
(Mr. *Gosar*) and the gentleman from Missouri (Mr. *Clay*) each will control 20 minutes.

The Chair recognizes the gentleman from Arizona.
GENERAL LEAVE
Mr. GOSAR. Mr. Speaker, I ask unanimous consent this all Members may have 5
legislative days within which to revise and extend their remarks and include extraneous material on the bill under consideration.

The SPEAKER pro tempore. Is there objection to the request of the gentleman from
Arizona?
There was no objection.

Mr. GOSAR. I yield myself such time as I may consume.

Mr. Speaker, H.R. 2338, introduced by the gentleman from Florida (Mr. *Posey*), would designate the facility of the United States Postal Service located at 600 Florida Avenue
in Cocoa, Florida, as the Harry T. and Harriette Moore Post Office. The bill is cosponsored by the entire Florida State delegation and was favorably reported by the Committee on Oversight and Government Reform on June 27.

Mr. Speaker, it is altogether fitting and proper that we name this post office in Cocoa, Florida, for Harry and Harriette Moore, leaders of the civil rights movement in Florida. Harry Moore established the first branch of the NAACP in Brevard County, Florida, and is considered the first martyr of the civil rights movement. Sadly, on Christmas night in 1951, the Moores were killed by a bomb planted beneath their home.

Mr. Speaker, I urge my colleagues to join me in strong support of this bill, and I reserve the balance of my time.

Mr. CLAY. I yield myself such time as I may consume. Mr. Speaker, I, too, want to join with my colleague from Arizona in consideration of H.R. 2338, to name the post office in Cocoa, Florida, after Harry T. and Harriette Moore. In accordance with committee requirements, H.R. 2338 is cosponsored by all members of the Florida delegation and was reported out of the Oversight Committee by unanimous consent. It honors the legacy of Harry T. and Harriette Moore, who both fought tirelessly for civil rights and against voter discrimination.

In 1934, Harry and Harriette organized the first NAACP branch, as was mentioned, in Brevard County. In the face of discrimination, the Moores succeeded in establishing additional NAACP branches throughout Florida. In addition, the Moores worked with the Progressive Voters League to register over 100,000 African Americans in the State. Harry's hard work and determination led him to become the president of the Florida State Conference of NAACP branches. Tragically, as was mentioned, in 1951, Harry and Harriette Moore were fatally injured when a bomb planted underneath their house exploded. The Moores were survived by their only daughter, Juanita.

Mr. Speaker, I urge the passage of this bill to commemorate the legacy of Harry T. and Harriette Moore, and I reserve the balance of my time.

Mr. GOSAR. I yield such time as he may consume to my distinguished colleague from the State of Florida (Mr. *Posey*), the sponsor of this legislation.

Mr. POSEY. I thank the gentleman for yielding.

Mr. Speaker, today we take an important step to honor the lives of Harry T. Moore and his wife, Harriette Moore. These leaders in the struggle for civil rights were taken from us 61 years ago this Christmas.

Harry T. and Harriette Moore propelled the struggle for justice and equality far beyond the borders of their home in Brevard County, Florida. Leaders in the modern civil rights movement, they are remembered for their dignity, compassion, and emphasis on education. They left a legacy that remains close to the hearts of community leaders and one that is sure to outlast the length of their lives that were so tragically cut short.

At a young age, the Moores were dedicated teachers and educators in our local community. Harry began his first job as an elementary teacher at Monroe Elementary School in Cocoa in 1925. Two years later, he began a decade of service as a high school principal in Titusville. Then, from 1936 to 1946, he served as a principal and fifth- and sixth-grade teacher at Mims.

The couple first met in Brevard County when Harry was serving as a principal in Titusville and Harriette was an elementary schoolteacher. They were married on Christmas Day in 1926, and were later blessed with two daughters. They committed the remainder of their lives to the pursuit of civil justice for African Americans.

The Moores first founded the Brevard County chapter of the NAACP in 1934,

[Page: H6483]
which led to a statewide NAACP conference in 1941. Mr. Moore served as president of the Florida State Conference of the NAACP chapters, as well as the founder and executive director of the Progressive Voters League, as was mentioned earlier.

It was through these channels that the Moores championed such issues as equality, education, and voter registration. But their steadfast adherence to equality was not without a price, as both Mr. and Mrs. Moore were fired from their teaching jobs and found it difficult to find employment. To proclaim them as pillars of the community would be an understatement.

The couple celebrated their 25th wedding anniversary on Christmas Eve 1951. As they celebrated, a bomb exploded beneath their home. Mr. Moore died on his way to the hospital, and Mrs. Moore died as a result of her injuries 9 days later.

[Time: 14:10]

The tragic murders sparked an even more resounding outcry for civil rights.

Harry T. Moore has been called the first American civil rights martyr. Brevard County has honored the Moores' deep impact on the community by designating their home site a Florida Historical Heritage Landmark, creating the Harry T. and Harriette Moore Memorial Park and Interpretive Center, and naming its Justice Center after the trailblazing couple.

Additionally, the NAACP posthumously awarded Mr. Moore the Spingarn Medal for outstanding achievement by an African American. Both these fine citizens undoubtedly touched the lives of others with the dedication, integrity, persistence, compassion, and commitment each of them so courageously demonstrated.

I am pleased that the U.S. House of Representatives is acting today to pass this legislation to name the U.S. Post Office in Cocoa, Florida, in honor of Harry T. and Harriette Moore. Passage of H.R. 2338 will further honor the achievements and sacrifices of the Moores, the leaders and first martyrs of our Nation's modern civil rights era.

Designating the United States Post Office at 600 Florida Avenue in Cocoa as the Harry T. and Harriette Moore Post Office will commemorate the Moores' legacy in a town where Mr. Moore began his service to others. This will serve as a constant reminder to our community of the important and lasting contributions the Moores made to Cocoa and the Nation.

I urge my colleagues to join me in passing this legislation.

Mr. CLAY. Mr. Speaker, let me thank and congratulate my good friend from Florida (Mr. *Posey*) for bringing to this House, bringing to our attention these two great Americans and the legacy that they left this country. Thank you for doing that.

Mr. Speaker, I have no further speakers, and I

yield back the balance of my time. Mr. GOSAR.

Mr. Speaker, I urge all Members to support the

passage of H.R. 2338,
and I yield back the balance of my time.

The SPEAKER pro tempore. The question is on the
motion offered by the gentleman from Arizona (Mr.
Gosar) that the House suspend the rules and pass
the bill, H.R. 2338.

The question was taken; and (two-thirds being
in the affirmative) the rules were suspended
and the bill was passed.

A motion to reconsider was laid on the table.

PICTURE GALLERY

From the earth his voice cries, No bomb can kill the dream I hold
For freedom never dies!

Figure 1 the Reconstructed House located at the Harry T. and
Harriette V. Moore Cultural Complex above an Inserted Picture
of the House following the Blast on Christmas Day 1951. A
Rendering of Harriette and Harry Moore displayed in the
Complex in Mims, Florida.

Figure 2 Harriette Carrying Baby Jaunita Evangeline with Harry Holding Peaches' Hands

Figure 3 Harry T. Moore as a Young Man

We seek no special favors; but certainly we have a right to expect justice and equal protection under the laws.

Harry T. Moore

Figure 4 Harry T. Moore Speaks Out

Figure 5 Annual Festival Remembers the Slain Heroes

Figure 6   Harry T. & Harriette V. Moore Memorial Park

Figure 8 Harry Holding Baby Jaunita Evangeline

Figure 7 Jaunita Evangeline Moore as a Young Woman

Figure 9 Peaches with Friends at Home